Lowercase Letter Tracing Workbook

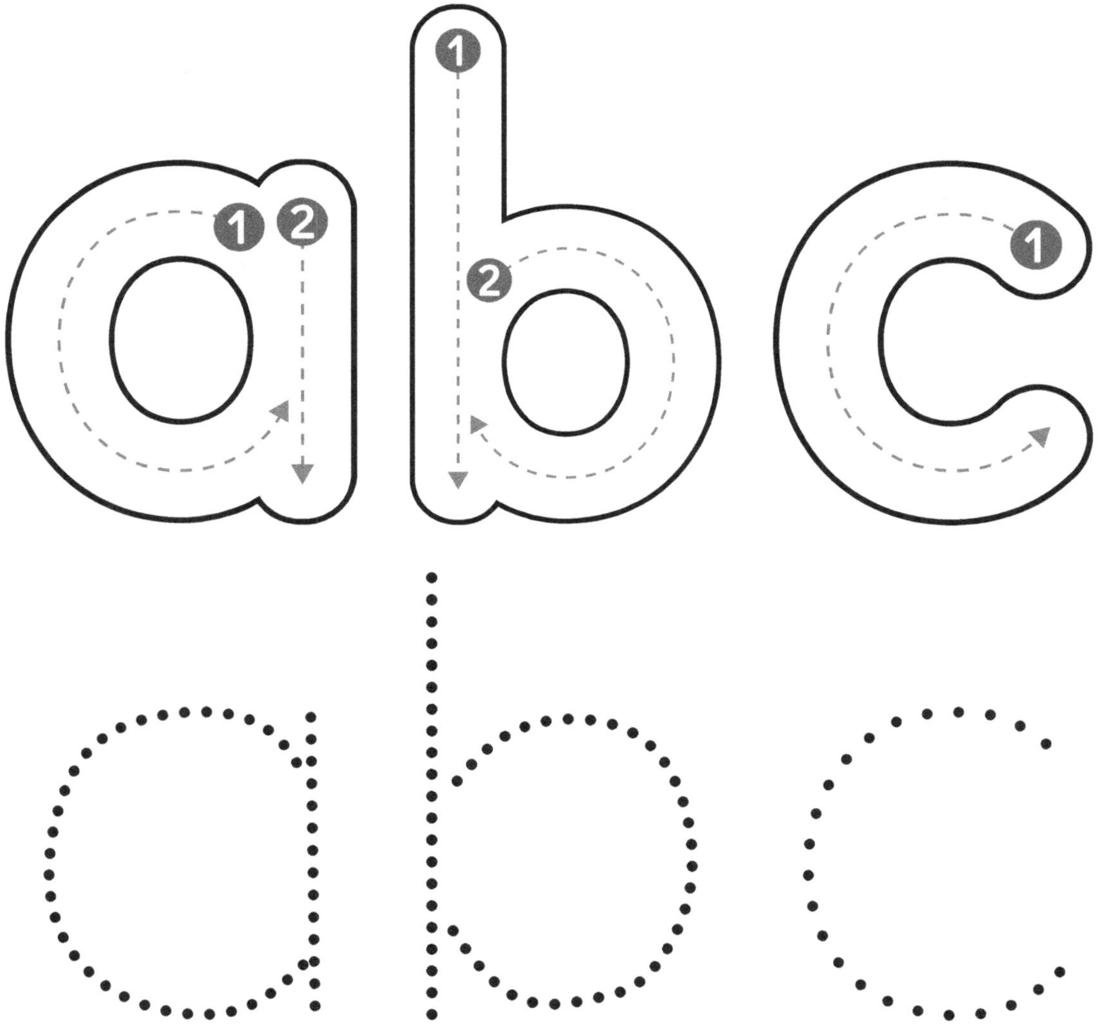

contact@siohanpress.com

ISBN 978-1-959451-00-6

Siohan Press

www.siohanpress.com

_____

Write your name above.

Let's get started!

Finger trace the letter

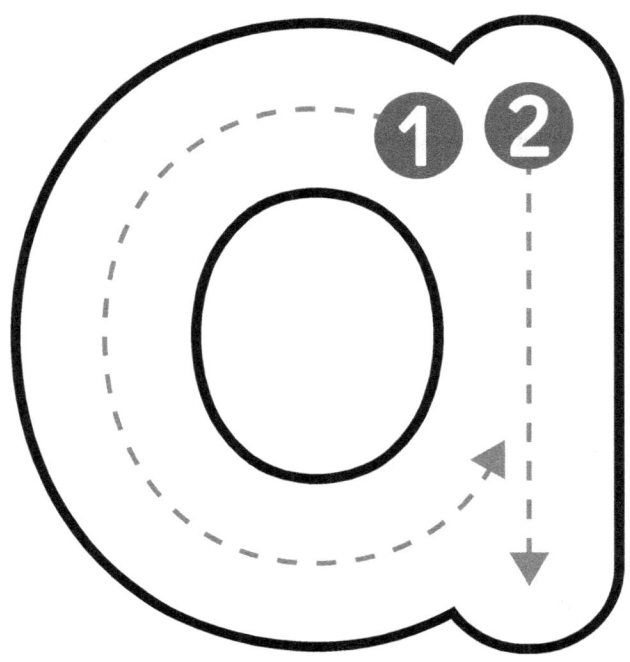

Trace the letters

Finger trace the letter

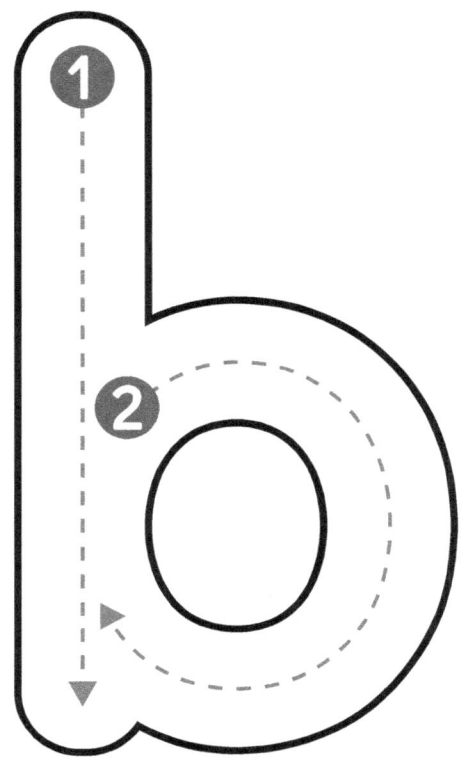

Trace the letters

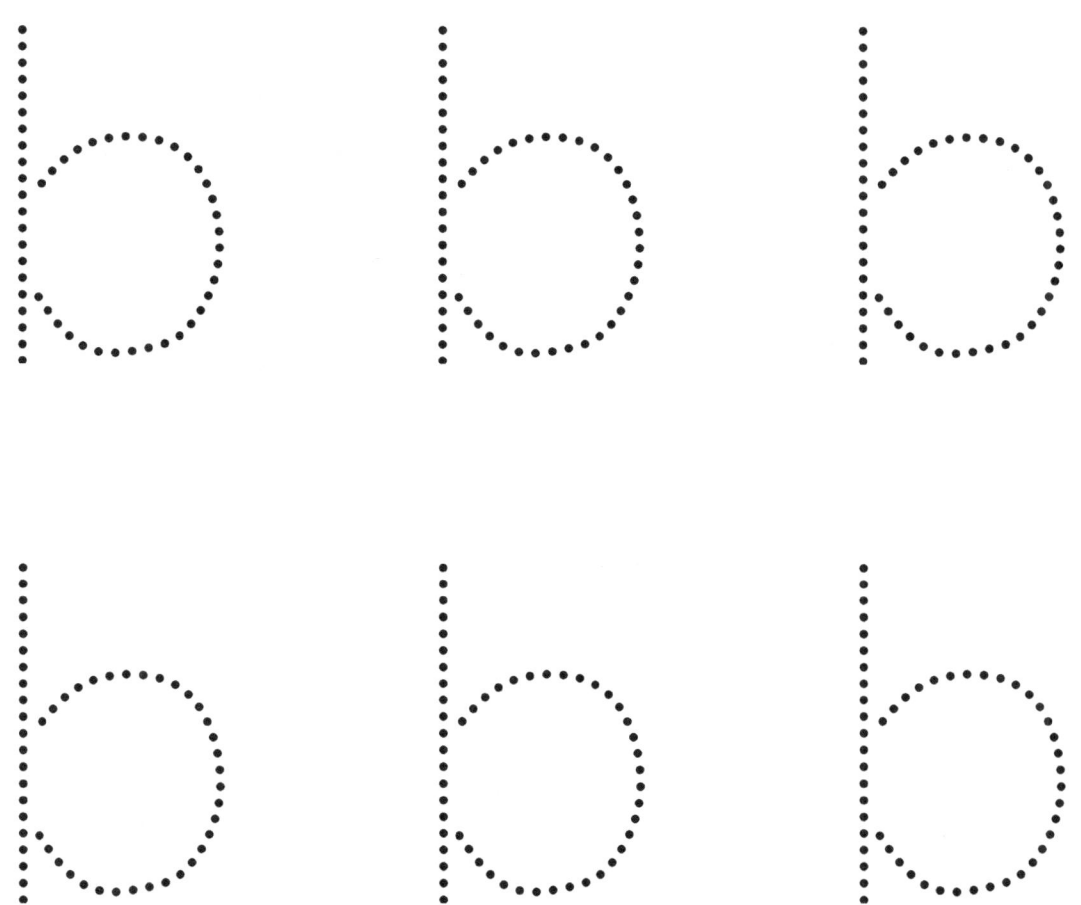

Finger trace the letter

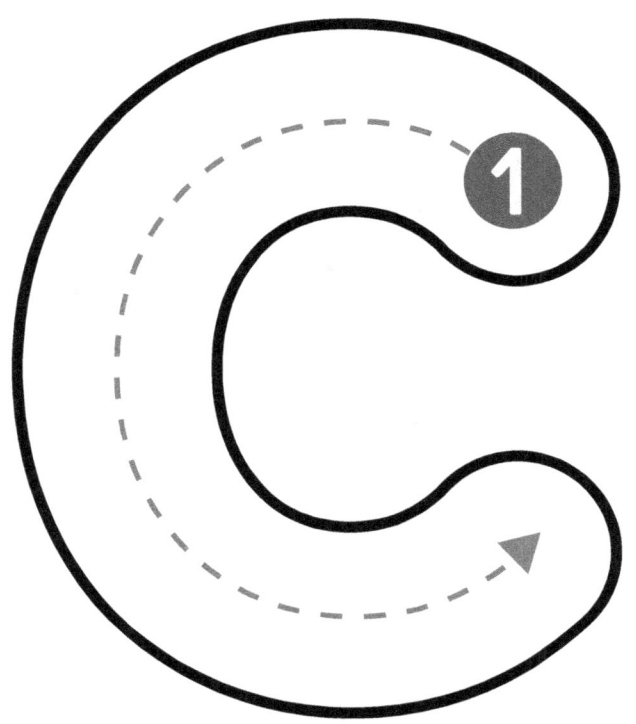

Trace the letters

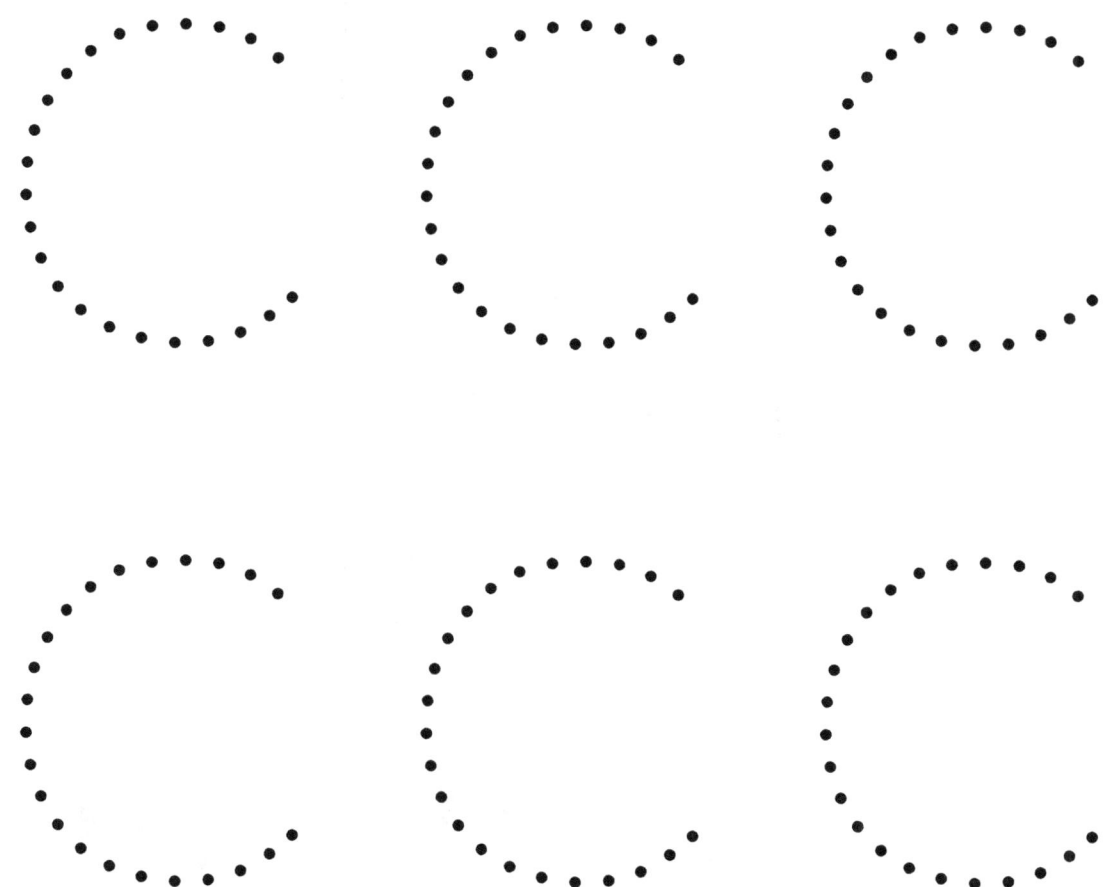

Finger trace the letter

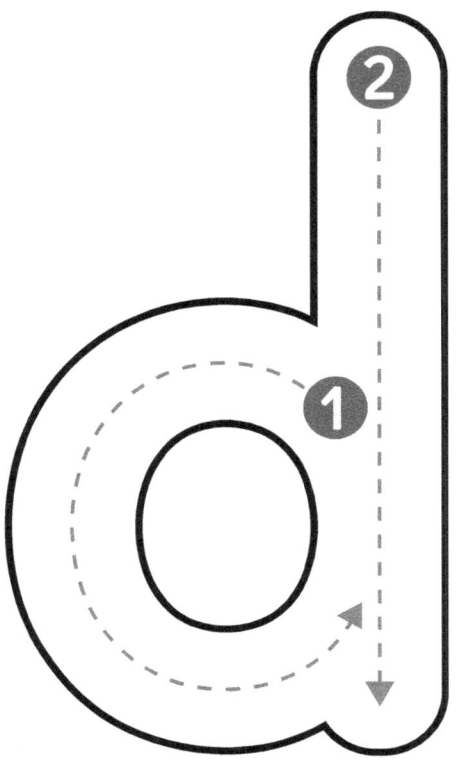

Trace the letters

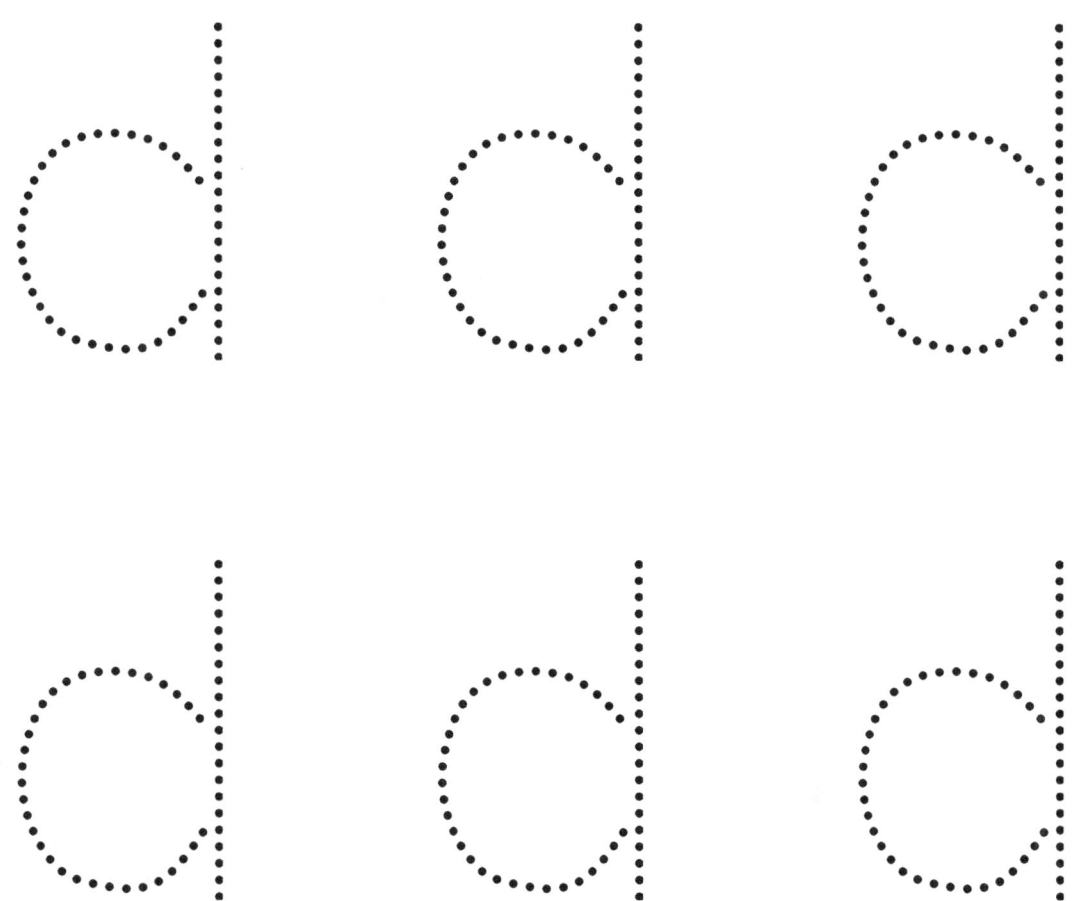

Finger trace the letter

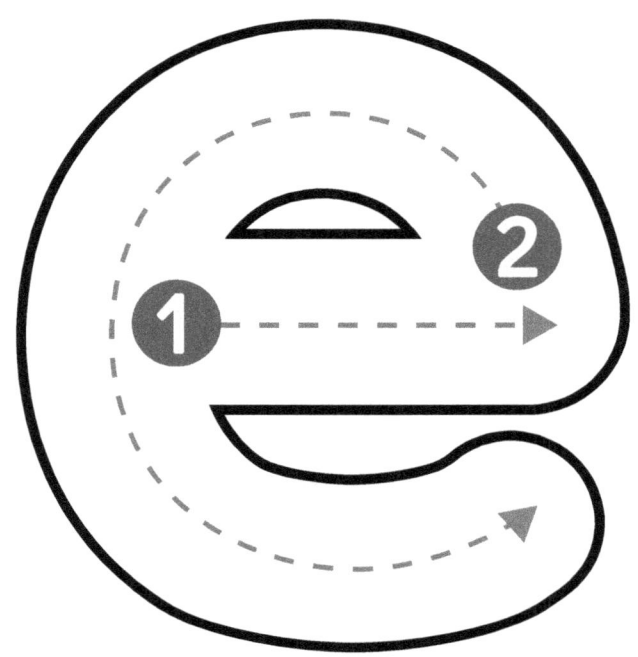

Trace the letters

Finger trace the letter

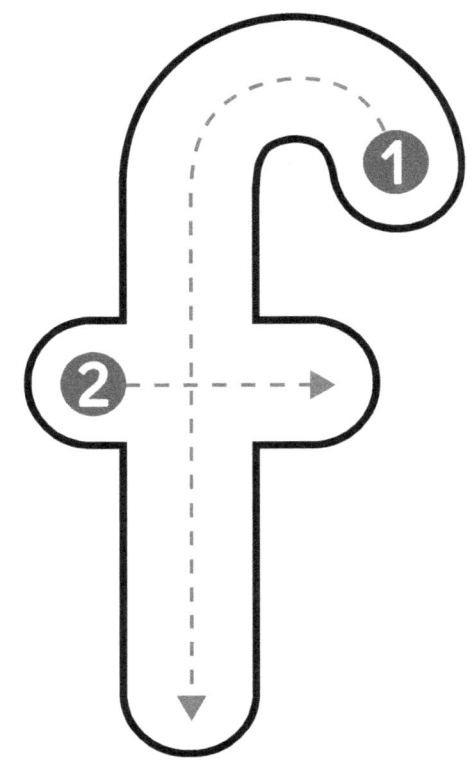

Trace the letters

Finger trace the letter

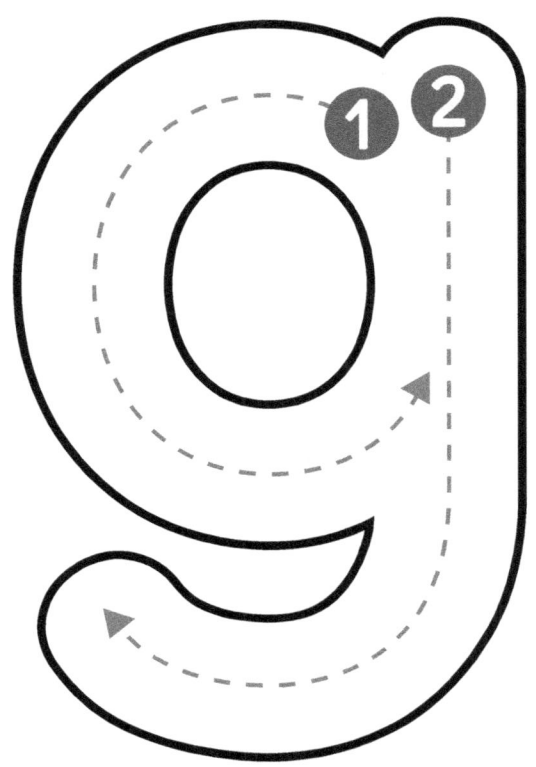

Trace the letters

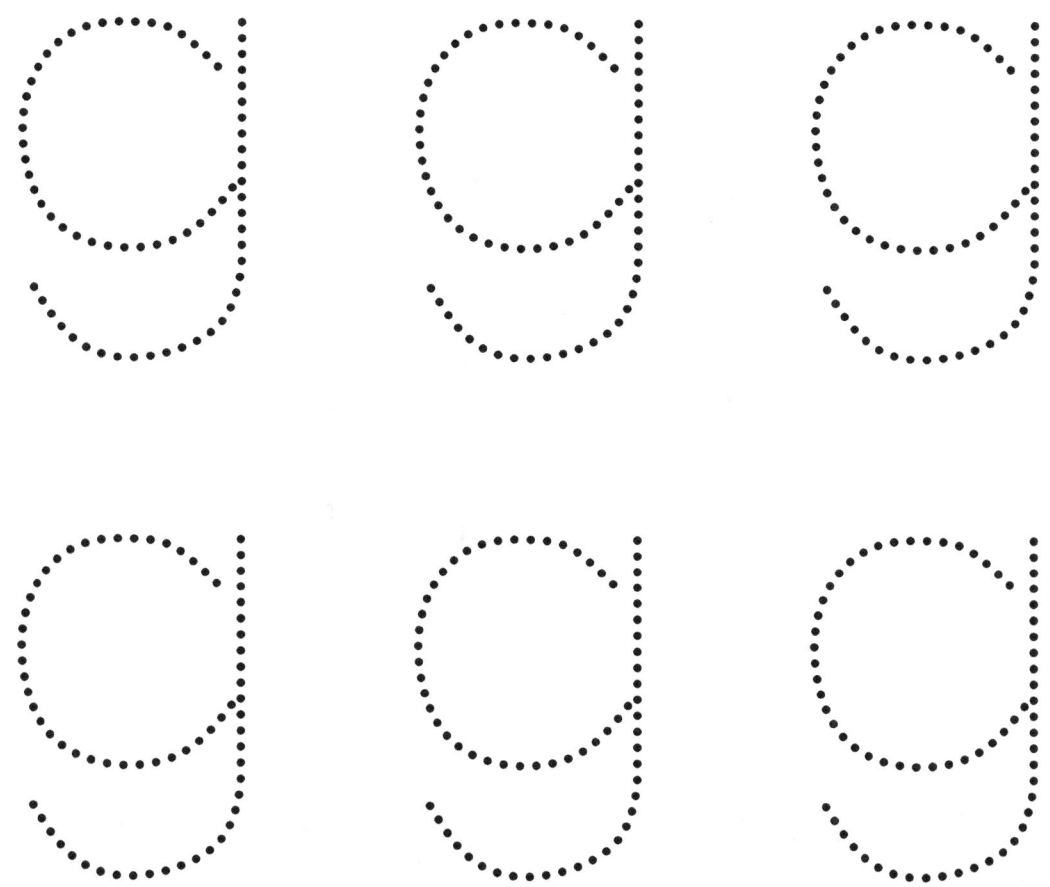

Finger trace the letter

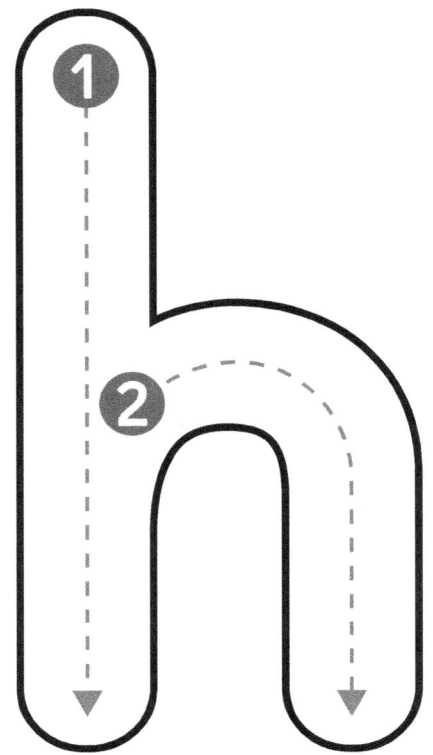

Trace the letters

Finger trace the letter

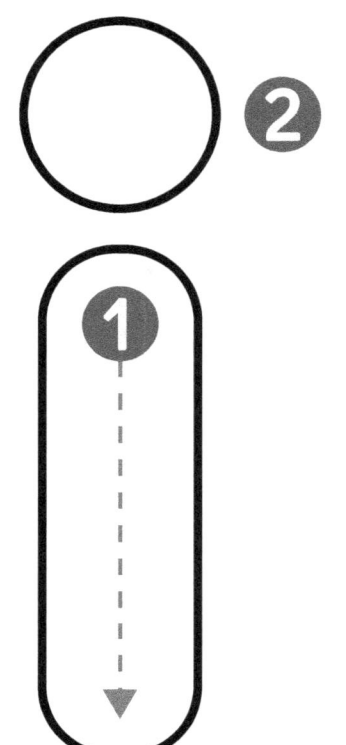

Trace the letters

Finger trace the letter

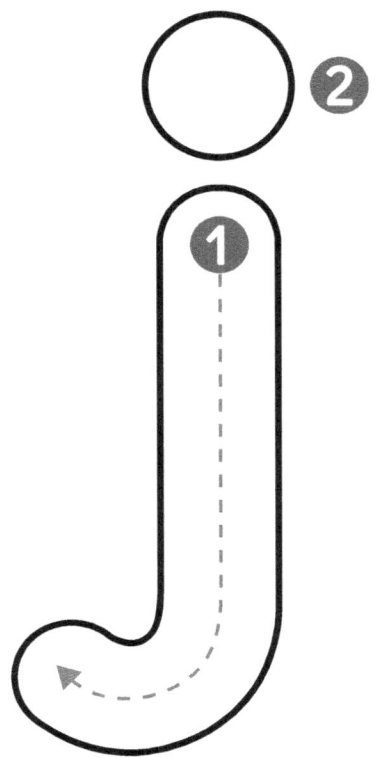

Trace the letters

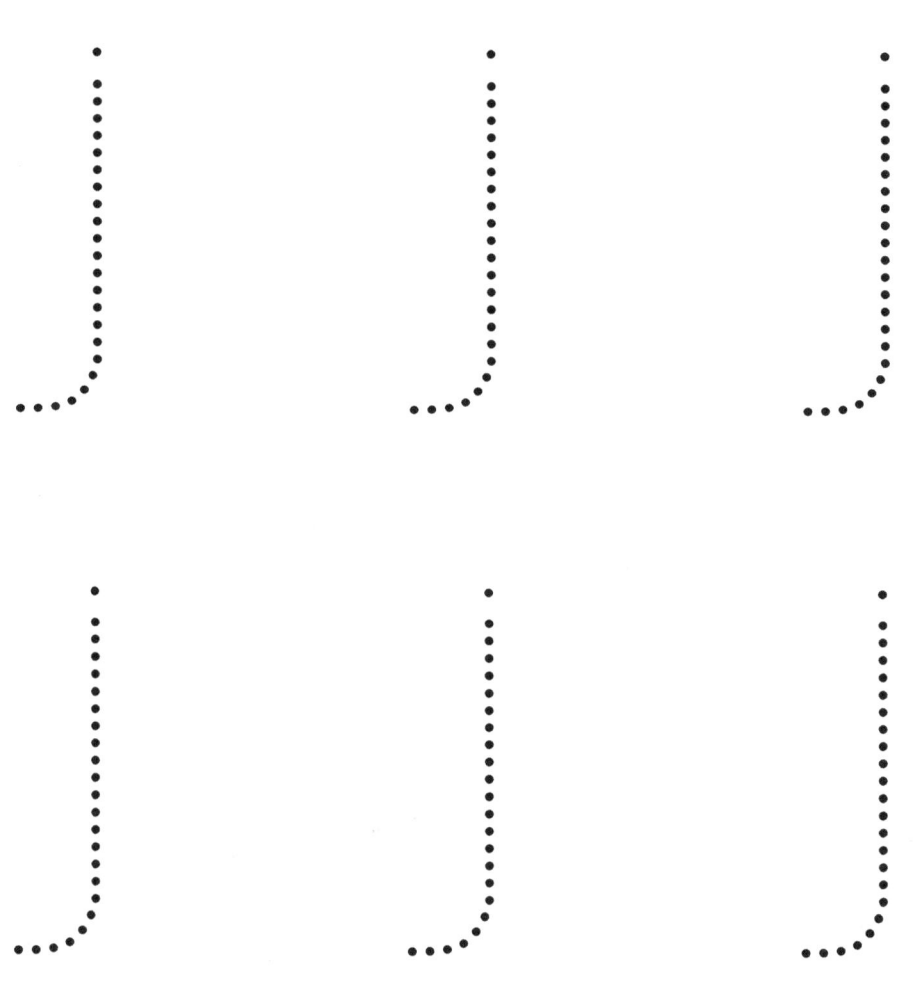

Finger trace the letter

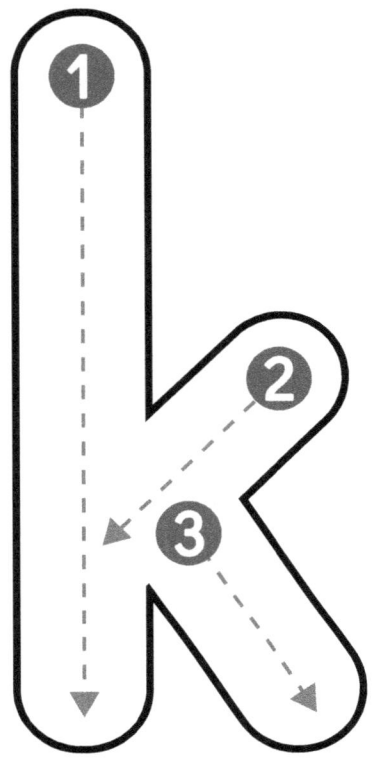

Trace the letters

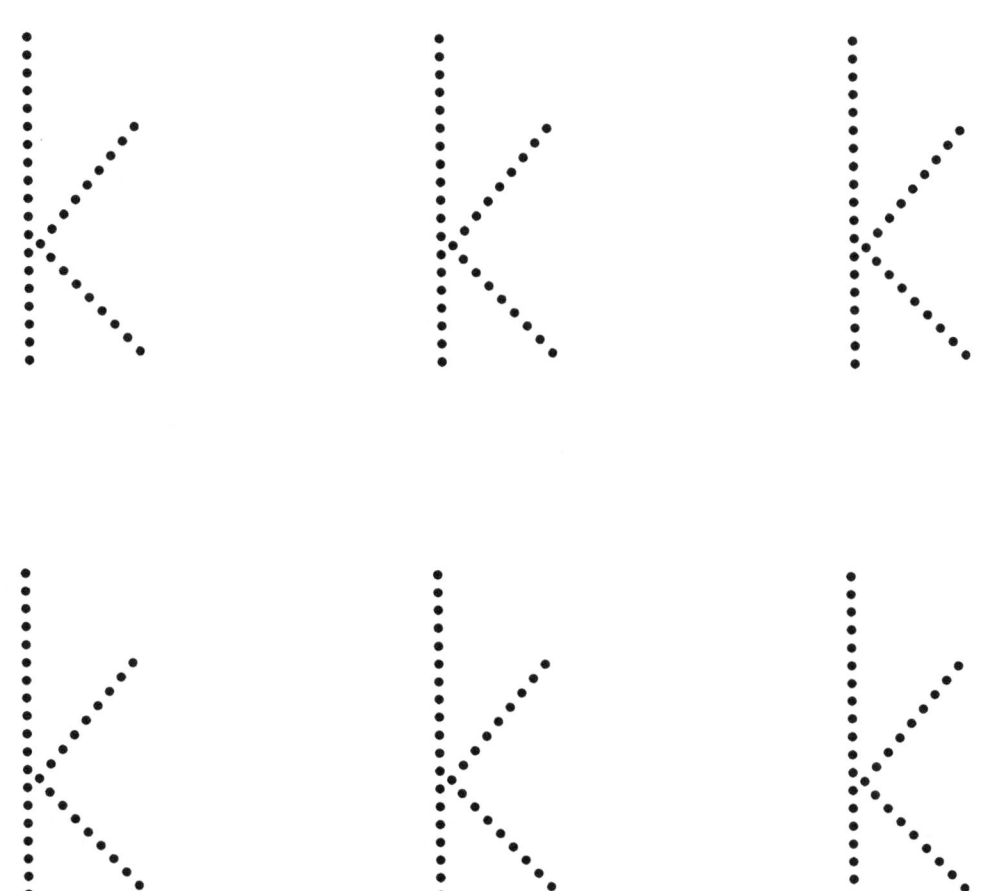

Finger trace the letter

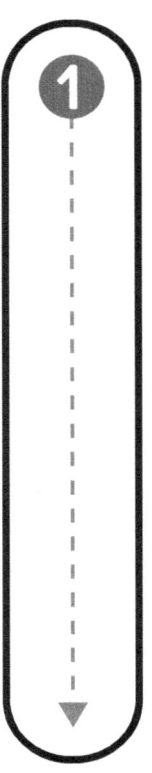

Trace the letters

Finger trace the letter

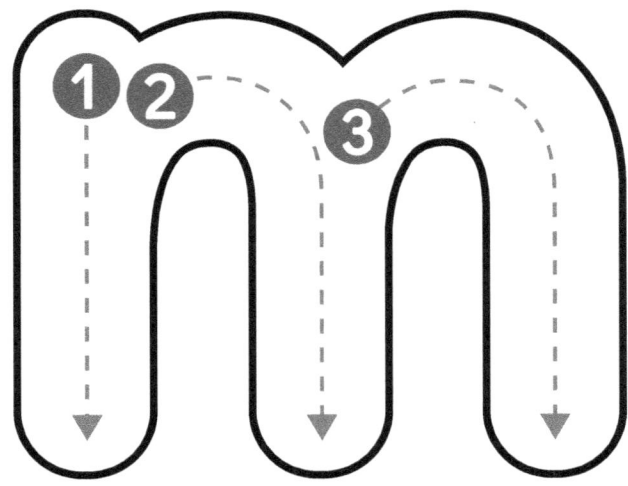

Trace the letters

Finger trace the letter

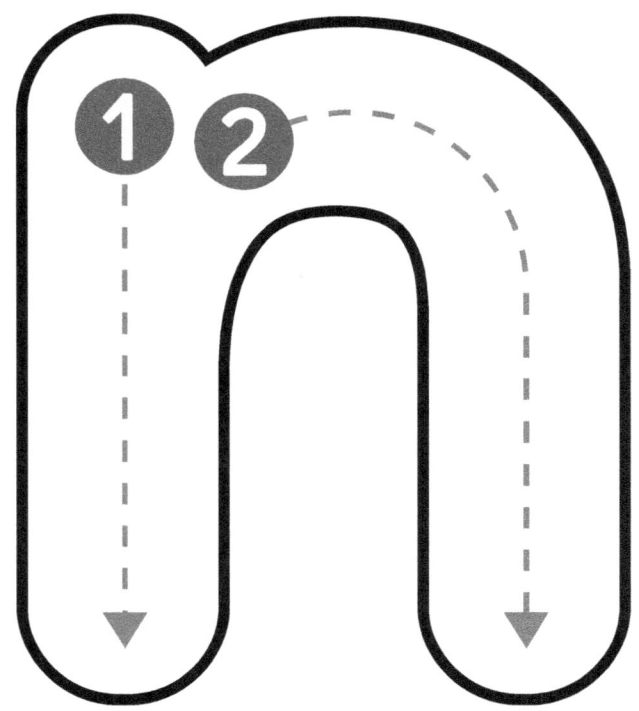

Trace the letters

Finger trace the letter

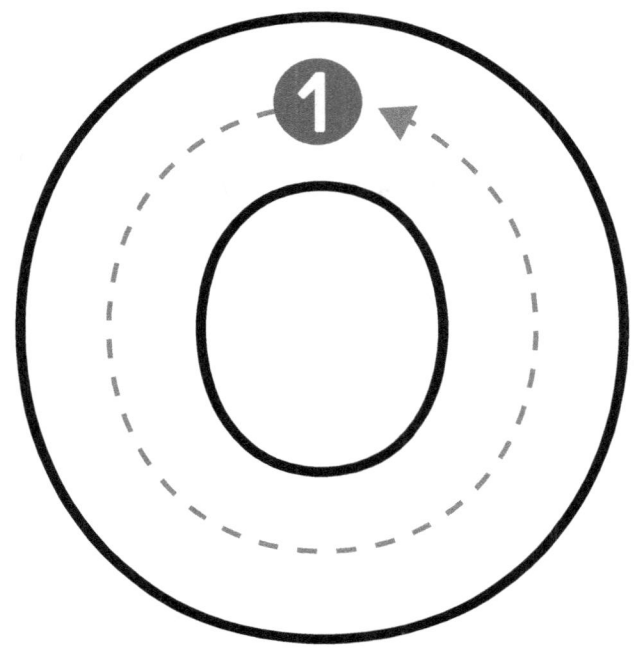

Trace the letters

Finger trace the letter

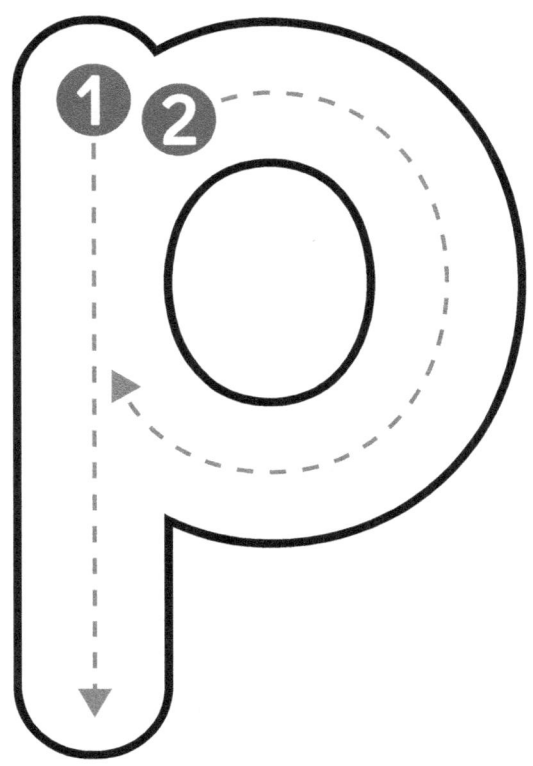

Trace the letters

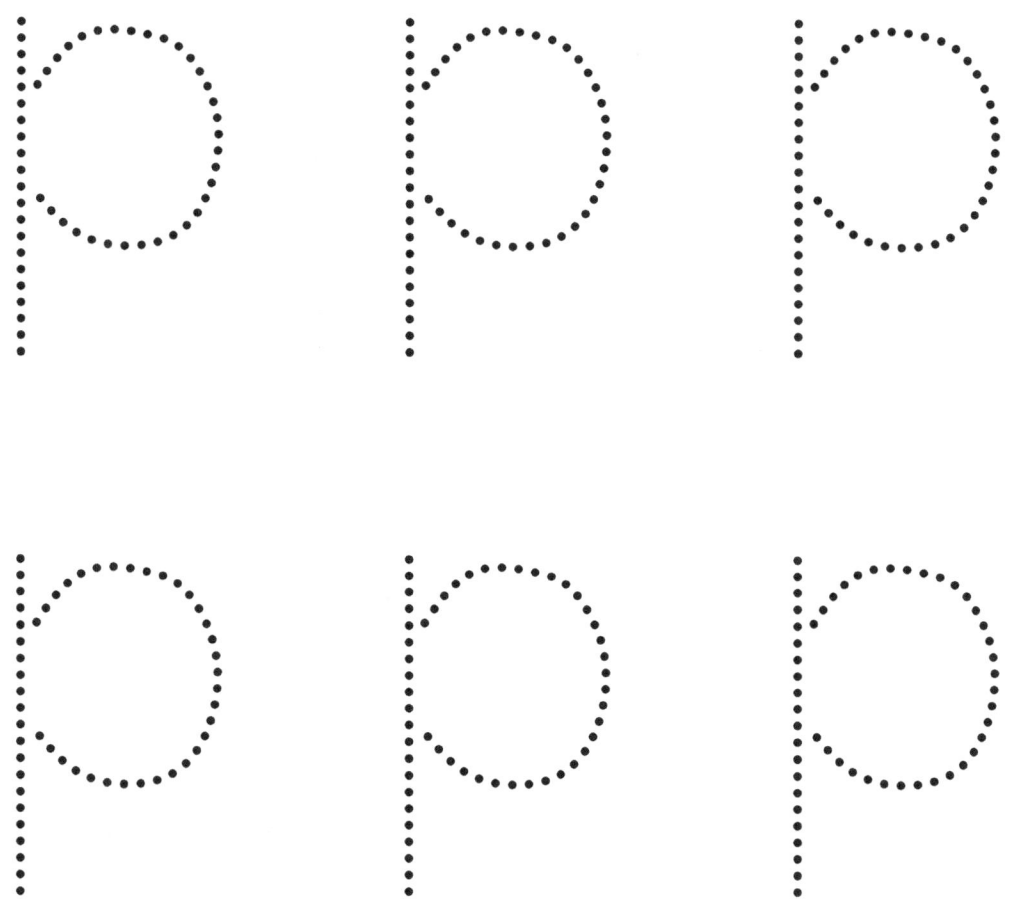

Finger trace the letter

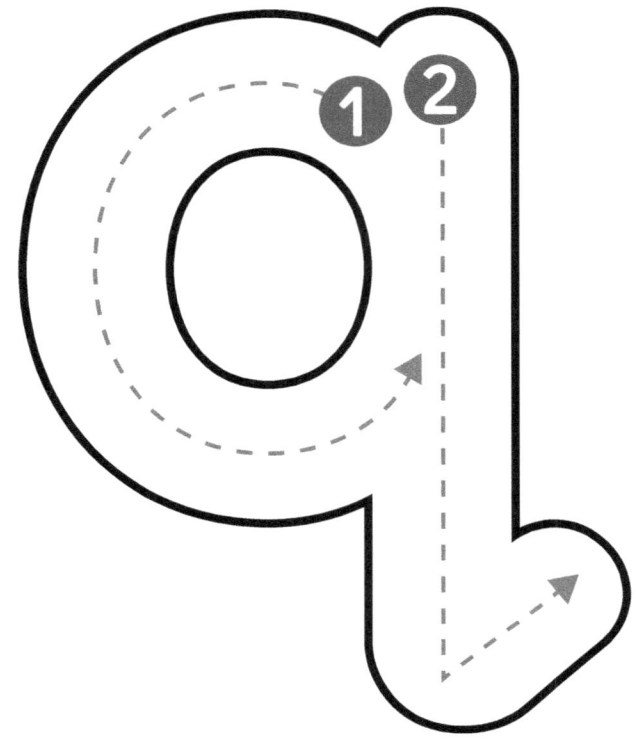

Trace the letters

Finger trace the letter

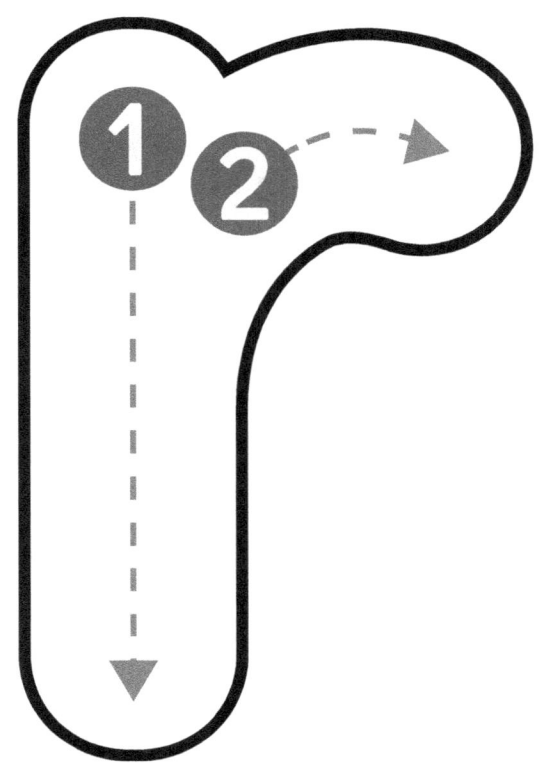

Trace the letters

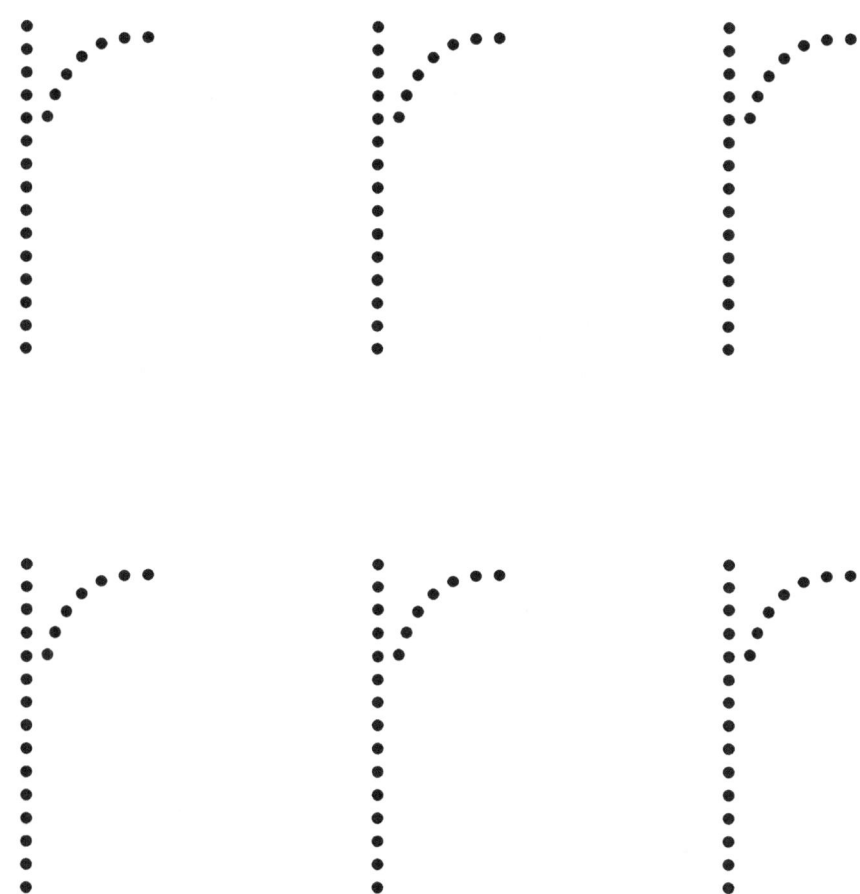

Finger trace the letter

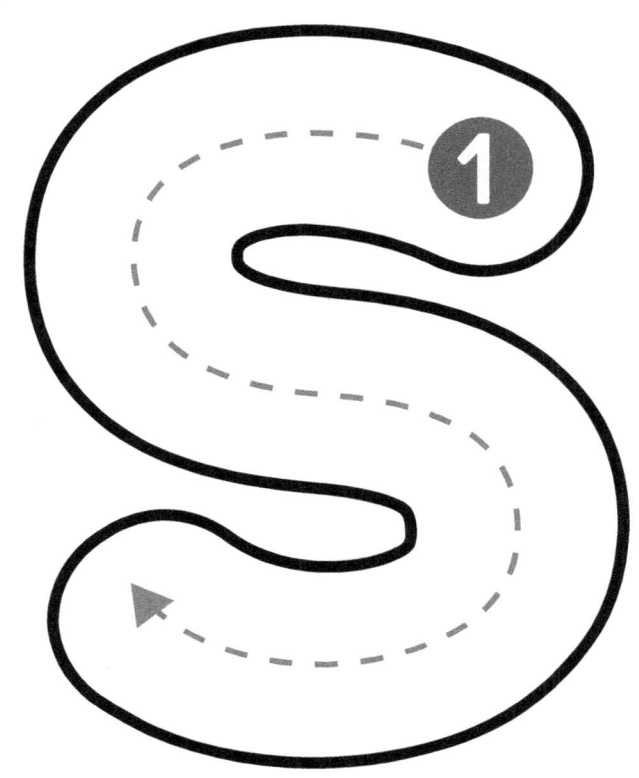

Trace the letters

Finger trace the letter

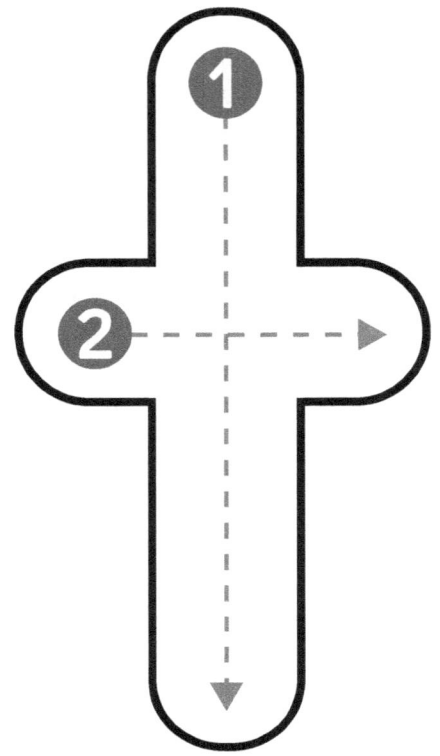

Trace the letters

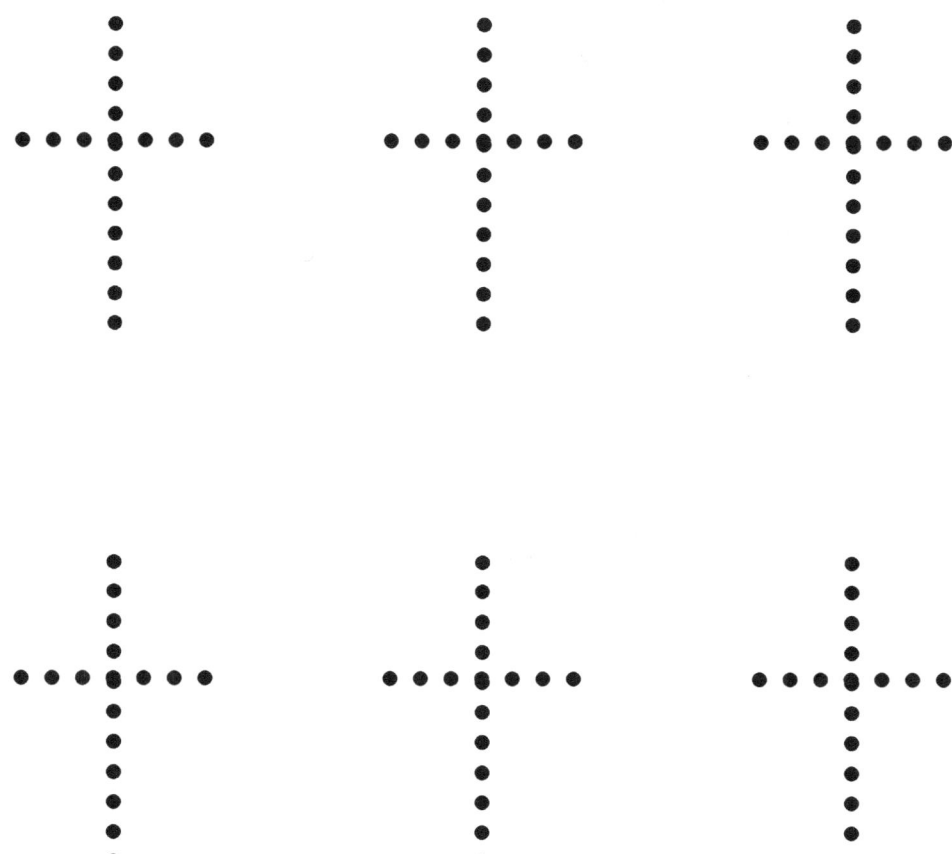

Finger trace the letter

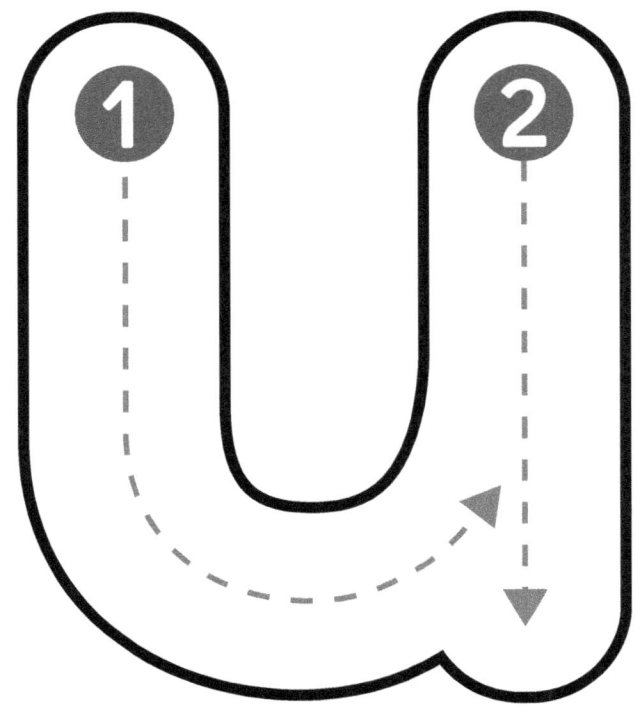

Trace the letters

Finger trace the letter

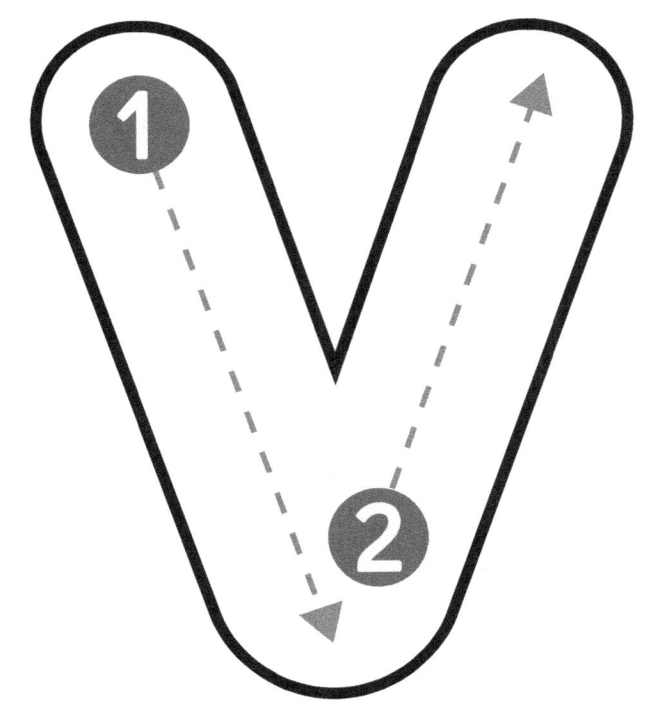

Trace the letters

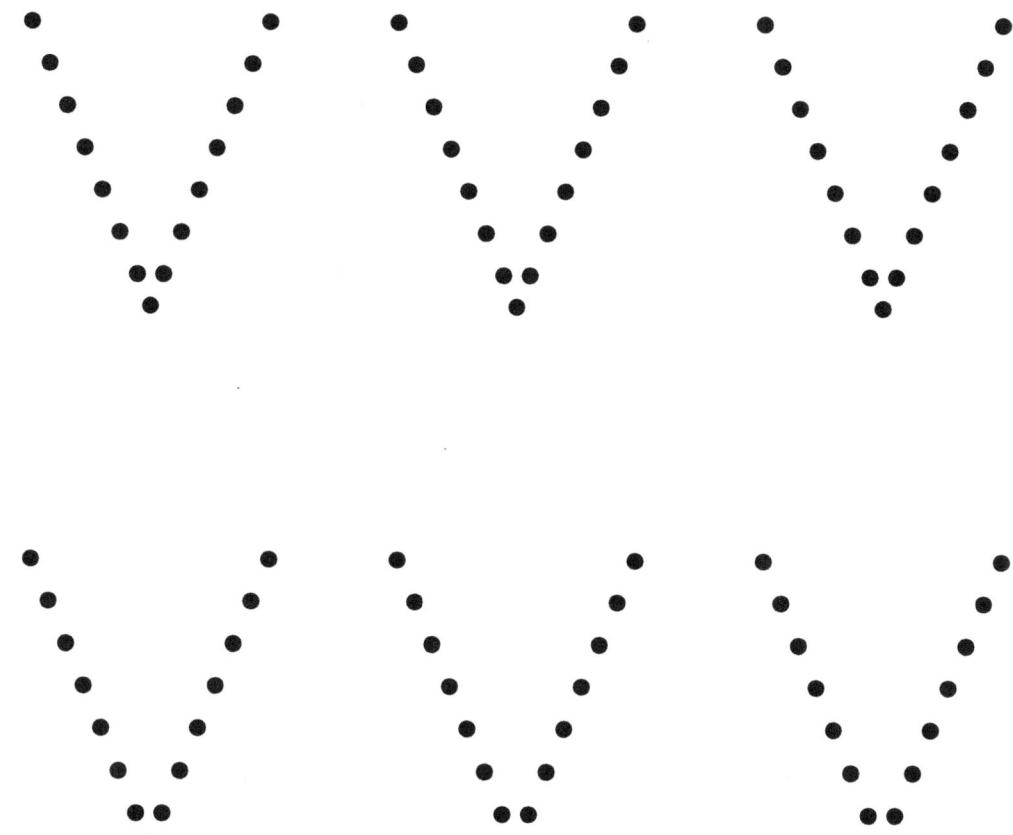

Finger trace the letter

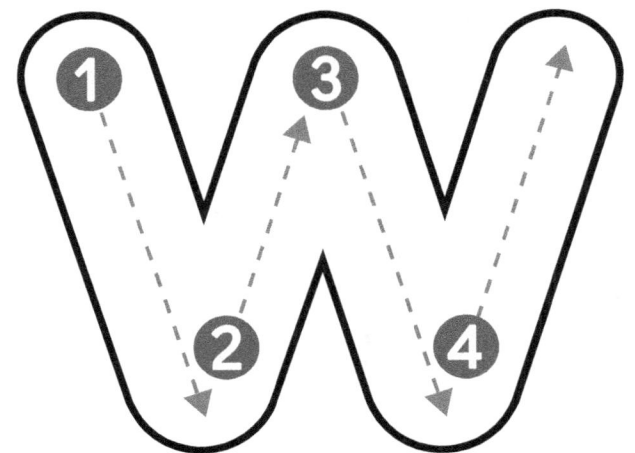

Trace the letters

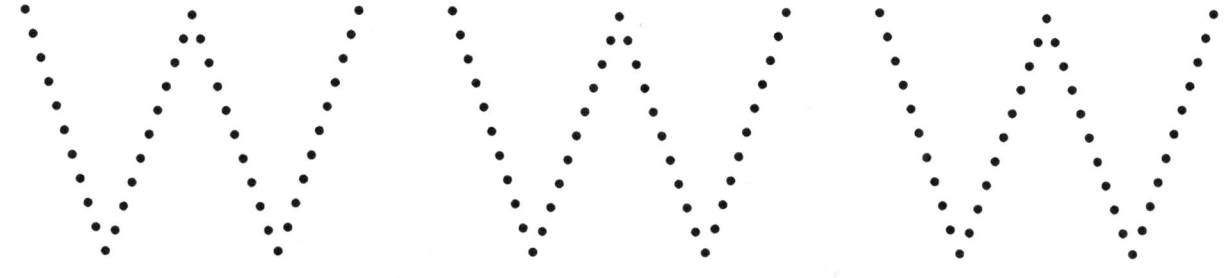

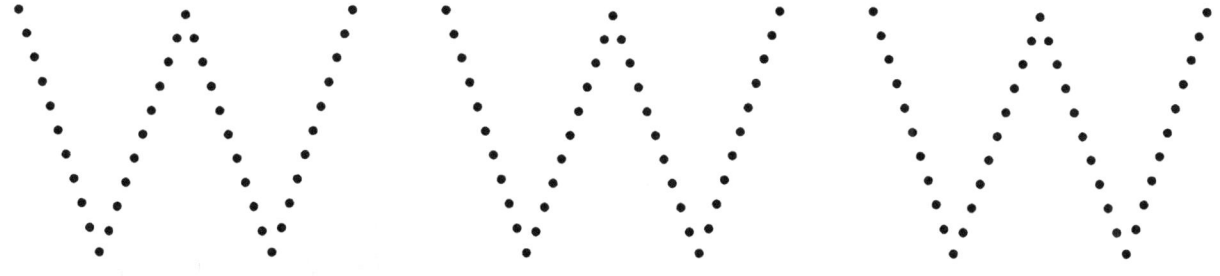

Finger trace the letter

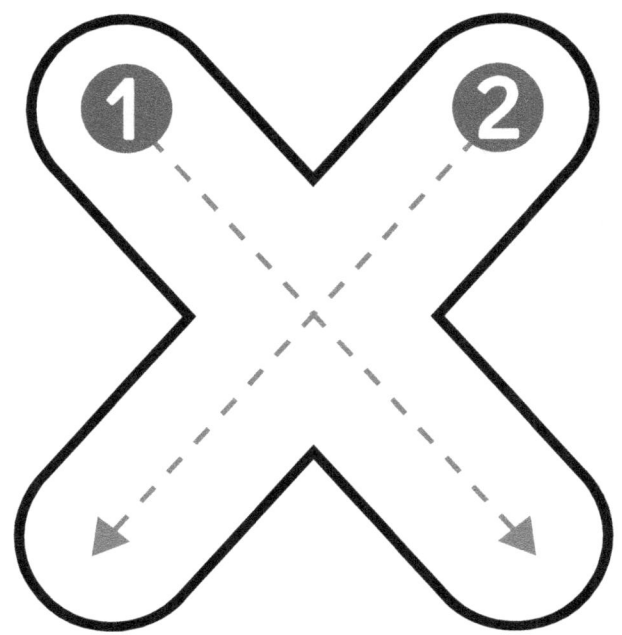

Trace the letters

Finger trace the letter

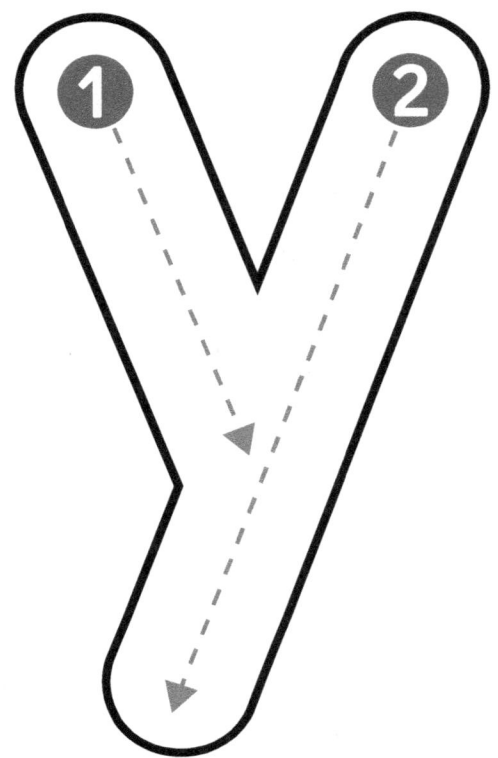

Trace the letters

Finger trace the letter

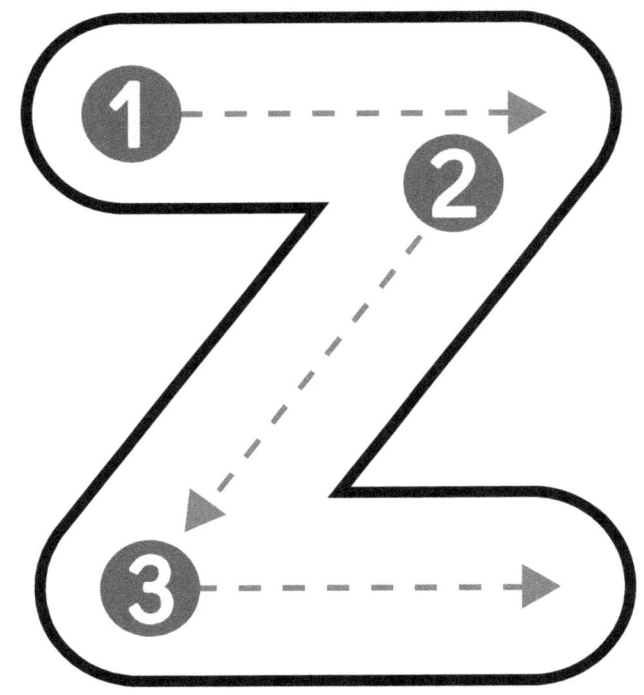

Trace the letters

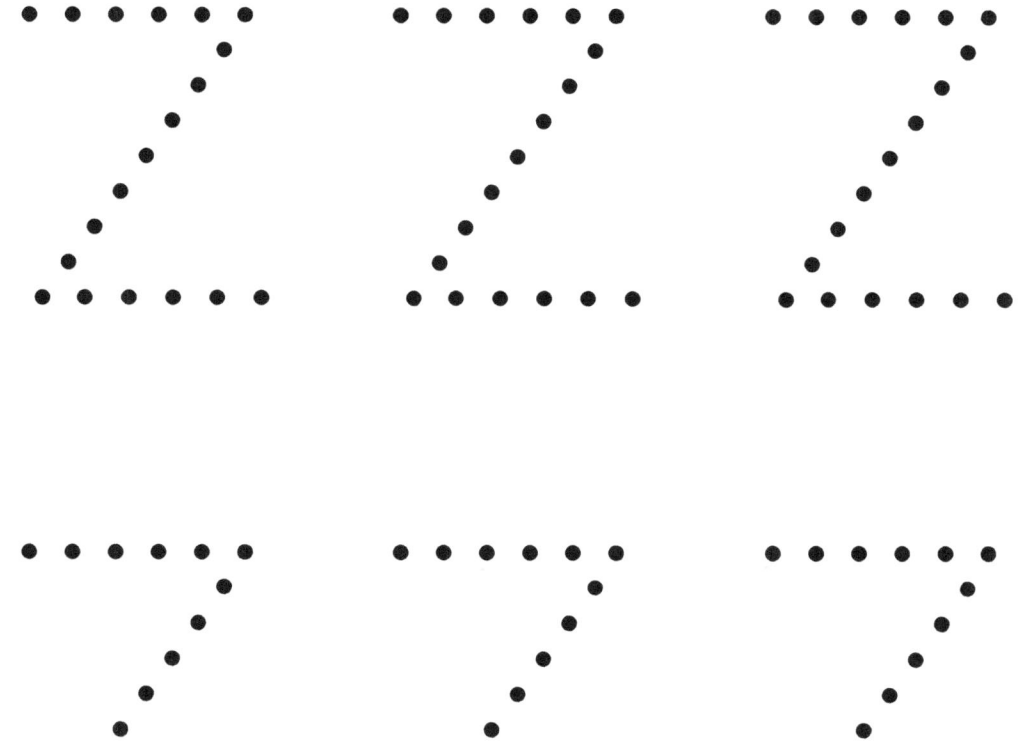

a b c d e

f g h i j k l

m n o p q

r s t u v

w x y z

Siohan Scholars presents
this certificate to

for completion of the

LOWERCASE LETTER
TRACING WORKBOOK

Check out more titles at www.siohanpress.com

www.ingramcontent.com/pod-product-compliance
Lightning Source LLC
Chambersburg PA
CBHW081009120626
46546CB00010B/3077